The Sun

Written by
Paulette Bourgeois

Illustrated by
Bill Slavin

Kids Can Press

Acknowledgments

I am grateful for the help of the scientists at the McLaughlin Planetarium at the Royal Ontario Museum, and the Ontario Science Centre for sending information and answering questions. I am thankful that Terence Dickinson, a man who knows more about the skies than almost anyone else, made the time to read my manuscripts and make helpful suggestions. Bill Slavin was very patient and did a spectacular job making the science come alive. And finally, I would like to thank Elizabeth MacLeod, a wonderful writer and editor, who always asked the right questions and kept me on track.

First U.S. edition 1997

CMC 95 0 9 8 7 6 5 4 3
CMC PA 96 0 9 8 7 6 5 4 3 2

Published in Canada by
Kids Can Press Ltd.
29 Birch Avenue
Toronto, ON M4V 1E2

Published in the U.S. by
Kids Can Press Ltd.
85 River Rock Drive, Suite 202
Buffalo, NY 14207

A story about the Sun's energy, page 33, adapted from *Tcakabesh Snares the Sun*, from THE MAN IN THE MOON by Alta Jablow and Carl Withers. Copyright © 1969 by Alta Jablow and Carl Withers. Illustrations copyright © 1969 by Peggy Wilson. Reprinted by permission of Henry Holt and Co., Inc.

Photo Credits
Bill Ivy: page 8, 14, 16, 17, 18, 24, 26, 28, 30, 32, 34, 37.
NASA: page 4, 6, 22, 31, 38

Canadian Cataloguing in Publication Data
Bourgeois, Paulette
        The sun

(Starting with space)
Includes index.
ISBN 1-55074-158-6 (bound)
ISBN 1-55074-330-9 (pbk.)

1. Sun — Juvenile literature. 2. Sun — Experiments — Juvenile literature. I. Slavin, Bill. II. Title. III. Series.

QB521.5.B67 1995   j523.7   C95-930757-5

Edited by Elizabeth MacLeod
Text design by Marie Bartholomew
Page layout and cover design by Esperança Melo
Printed in Hong Kong by Wing King Tong Co. Ltd.

Contents

The Sun: Earth's star

Ancient people knew the Sun brought light and warmth. But they didn't know what made it shine and where it went each night. So they made up stories to help them understand the secrets of the Sun.

Sun tales

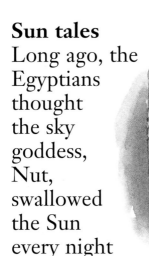

Long ago, the Egyptians thought the sky goddess, Nut, swallowed the Sun every night and gave birth to a new Sun the next morning.

People in Lithuania in eastern Europe told a different story. The Sun and Moon fell in love and got married. They had a baby and named her Earth. But the parents were always fighting. The Moon told the Sun to stop being so hot. The Sun told the Moon to stop being cold. They decided to separate.

But they both wanted to keep Earth. When they couldn't decide what to do, they visited the great god Thunder. Thunder told the Sun to take care of her daughter from morning until night and told the Moon to take care of Earth during the night.

And that's the way it's always been. Once in a while, when the Moon is too busy, his sisters, the stars, shine on Earth.

If you see a word you don't know, look it up in the glossary on page 39.

What is the Sun?

The Sun is a star — a bright, big ball of burning gas. It seems much larger than any other star because it is so much closer. The Sun is 150 million km (93 million miles) away from Earth. That seems like a long way but if the Sun were closer, nothing on Earth could survive the heat.

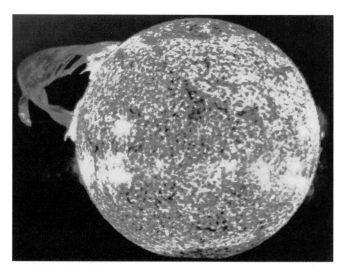

Here is one of the biggest solar flares ever.

SUN FACTS

The Sun measures 1 392 000 km (865 000 miles) across. If the Sun were an empty ball you could fit one million Earths inside it.

The Sun weighs 2 billion billion billion t (tons). That's 2 with 27 zeros after it. That's 333 000 times as much as Earth!

The Sun's gravity is 28 times greater than Earth's. If you weigh 45 kg (100 pounds) on Earth, you'd weigh almost 1.5 t (tons) on the Sun!

The Sun is 4½ billion years old.

How big a star is the Sun?

The Sun is a medium-sized star. Scientists say stars come in all sizes — anywhere from dwarf to giant size. They can be almost as small as Earth or 40 times as big as the Sun. Stars can glow blue (which means they are very hot), white, yellow or red (much cooler). Scientists call our Sun a yellow dwarf.

What does the Sun do?

The Sun gives us light and heat. The Sun's light makes plants grow. Plants give us food to eat and oxygen to breathe. We would die without them.

The Sun's heat gives us rain. When the Sun warms lakes and oceans some of the water changes into a gas called water vapor. This gas floats high in the sky to where the air is cooler. The water vapor is chilled and changes back into water drops. When a lot of these drops join together, they form clouds. If the water drops get large enough, they fall as rain.

The Sun's heat also gives us wind. The heat warms the air and when air is warm, it moves. And wind is moving air.

If there were no Sun, Earth would have no wind, rain, heat or light.

When did the Sun start to shine?
The Sun started to shine 4½
billion years ago.

Long, long before that, there
were nothing but gases floating
around in the universe. About 12
billion years ago, pockets of gas
gathered together to form the
Milky Way galaxy. Over time,
hundreds of billions of stars
were born inside the Milky Way.

Our Sun was one of those stars.
It started as an enormous cool
cloud of gas and dust. It became
smaller and hotter until it started
to shine.

Will the Sun shine forever?
No, all stars die. In about 5 billion years the Sun will start to glow red and grow bigger. It will become so hot that the ice at Earth's North Pole will melt and the oceans will begin to boil. The Sun will continue to grow until it swallows the planets closest to it — including Earth! Then the Sun will begin to shrink and become dimmer and dimmer until it is a small, dim star called a white dwarf.

Sun stuff

The solar system is the name given to the Sun and everything that travels around it, including the planets and their moons. Solar means "about the sun."

Why does the Sun shine?
It all starts in the Sun's center, also known as its core. The Sun's core is super hot, hotter than any furnace on Earth. And all the weight of the huge, heavy Sun presses on its core. The Sun is mostly made of hydrogen gas and near the core that gas becomes super hot and super squished. That makes the hydrogen turn into helium gas and give off huge blasts of energy as it changes.

Every second, 4 million tons of hydrogen change into helium and energy. But don't worry about the Sun using up all its hydrogen.

There is enough hydrogen in the Sun to keep it shining for another 5 billion years.

The energy the Sun makes as the hydrogen changes to helium starts moving from the Sun's core toward the outside. But because the Sun is so large and heavy, it takes millions of years for the energy to pass through it. When the energy finally reaches the Sun's surface, some of it turns into waves of light and heat that move outward very quickly through the emptiness of space. On Earth you can see the Sun's light waves, or sunshine, and you can feel the heat waves.

Sun stuff

Light takes only 8 minutes and 20 seconds to zoom from the Sun to Earth. The fastest jet on Earth would take a million times that long. Some stars you see at night are so far away that their light takes 4000 years to reach us!

What does the Sun look like?

You should never look at the Sun, not even with strong sunglasses. Your eyes focus the Sun's light onto a small spot inside them. That makes the light strong enough to burn your eyes and make you blind. However, scientists have machines that let them look at the Sun so they can see its different parts.

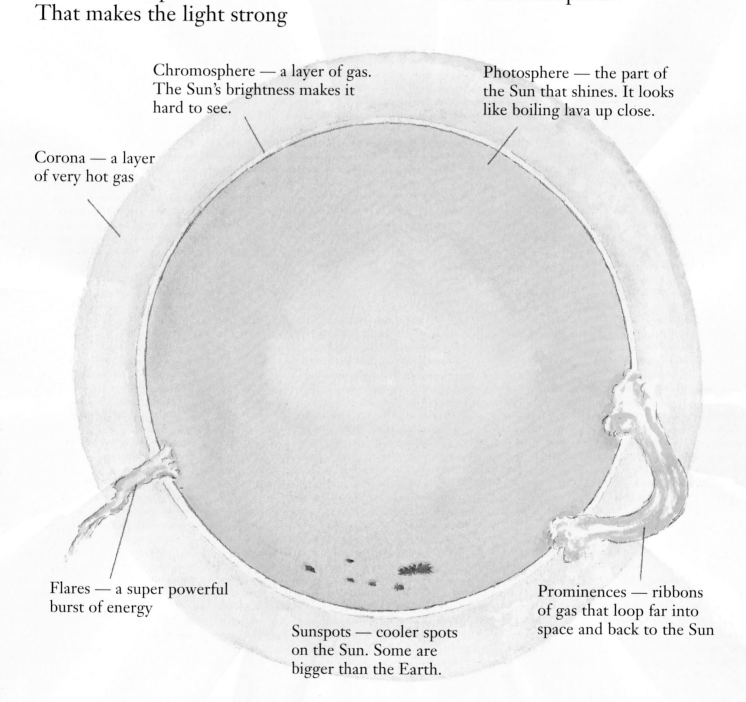

Chromosphere — a layer of gas. The Sun's brightness makes it hard to see.

Photosphere — the part of the Sun that shines. It looks like boiling lava up close.

Corona — a layer of very hot gas

Flares — a super powerful burst of energy

Sunspots — cooler spots on the Sun. Some are bigger than the Earth.

Prominences — ribbons of gas that loop far into space and back to the Sun

The parts of the Sun

TRY IT!

Look at the Sun safely

You'll need:
○ a sunny day
○ tape
○ a large piece of white paper
○ a small square of cardboard
○ a small nail
○ a stake or stick
○ a bucket of sand
○ a mirror
○ an adult helper

1. Tape the paper to a wall outside.

2. Have an adult punch a hole in the center of the cardboard with the nail. Tape the cardboard to the stick — don't put the hole in front of the stick!

3. Stand the stick in the bucket of sand. Place the bucket in front of the paper on the wall.

4. Ask a friend to hold the mirror and move it until it reflects the Sun through the hole in the cardboard. Look at the white paper until you see an image of the Sun. Draw what you see.

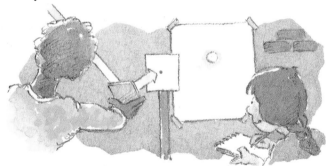

Looking at the Sun this way is a safe way to get an idea of how the Sun looks. Did you see any dark spots on the Sun? These are sunspots. Repeat this project a few days later and compare your pictures. You'll see that not all the sunspots are in the same place in both pictures. That's because sunspots move as the Sun spins.

Following the Sun

Long ago, people kept track of the seasons by
following the Sun.
They knew that in summer the Sun was high in the sky.
In winter it was much lower.
By watching the Sun, people knew when to gather food
for winter or to prepare for yearly rains or droughts.
And they all told stories about why there are seasons.

A story about the seasons

In ancient Greek stories, a beautiful goddess named Demeter looked after Earth. She especially loved harvest time, while her daughter, Persephone, loved the flowers of spring.

Below the surface of the Earth lived a god named Hades. His land was dark and gloomy. He kidnapped Persephone because he wanted her brightness to light his world. Demeter missed her daughter so much that she stopped caring for Earth. It began to dry up. Plants died and people were starving.

Demeter told the gods she could not look after Earth until her daughter came home. So Zeus, the father of the heavens, told Hades to return Persephone to her mother. But Zeus had one rule. If Persephone had eaten any food from the underworld, she could not return.

When Demeter saw her daughter again she was so happy that flowers bloomed. Then the sad truth came out. Persephone had eaten four pomegranate seeds while with Hades. She must go back to him. That meant Earth would die, and Zeus could not bear that. He decided Persephone would live with Hades for four months each year, one month for every seed.

Ever since, Earth is cold and dark while Persephone is away from Demeter. But as soon as she returns, there are spring flowers and sunshine. Mother and daughter spend summer together but as the time comes for Persephone to leave, plants start to die and Earth gets colder.

Why do we have seasons?

When it's summer where you live, the Sun is shining almost directly on you. The weather turns cold when the Sun's light shines on you from an angle. Then you get winter.

The seasons change because Earth leans to one side as it orbits, or circles, the Sun. As Earth makes one complete orbit around the Sun, your part of the world is either leaning toward the Sun or away from the Sun. People who live near the equator do not have seasons because they always get almost direct rays from the Sun.

When it is winter in the Northern hemisphere, it is summer in the Southern hemisphere.

The path a planet takes around the Sun is called its orbit. Earth takes 1 year, or 365 days and 6 hours, to make 1 orbit. Every 4 years those extra hours add up to a whole day and that day is added to the end of February. This special 366-day year is called a leap year.

What is a solstice?

A solstice takes place twice a year when the midday Sun is as low or as high in the sky as it can be. One solstice happens around December 21 and, north of the equator, it's known as the winter solstice. The other solstice takes place around June 21 and is called the summer solstice in the Northern hemisphere.

On the winter solstice, your part of the world is leaning as far away from the Sun as possible. This is known as the shortest day of the year because there are fewer hours of daylight than on any other day.

At the summer solstice, your part of the world leans as close to the Sun as possible. On that day you receive more hours of daylight than any other day. It's known as the longest day of the year. When it is the winter solstice in the Northern hemisphere, it is the summer solstice in the Southern hemisphere.

The first day of spring or fall is called the equinox. On these days, there are 12 hours of daylight and 12 hours of night.

Why do we have day and night?
If it is day where you live, your part of the world is facing the Sun. When night falls, your part of the world faces away from the Sun. This happens because every 24 hours Earth spins — or rotates — like a slowly spinning top. Half of the world is in sunlight while the other half is in darkness.

The Sun rises in the eastern part of the sky and sets in the west. At noon, your shadow points north if you are above the equator and south if you are below it.

During the summer the Sun is higher in the sky than it is in winter. The time between sunrise and sunset is longer, too. If you lived near the North Pole, you would see the Sun all night and all day in the middle of summer and you wouldn't see the Sun at all in the middle of winter.

At sunrise, your part of the world is beginning to face the Sun.

TRY IT!
Cast a big shadow

Plan to start this project early in the morning. You'll need to come back to spend a few minutes with it throughout the day.

> **You'll need:**
> - a sunny day
> - a large, open space such as a school yard
> - a friend
> - a piece of chalk
> - a measuring tape or measuring stick

1. In the early morning, ask your friend to stand in a sunny place. Trace around your friend's shadow. Measure the length of the shadow. Make a note of the time you do this.

2. Repeat step 1 about every two hours until late in the day.

3. Look at your shadow pictures and measurements. When is the shadow the longest?

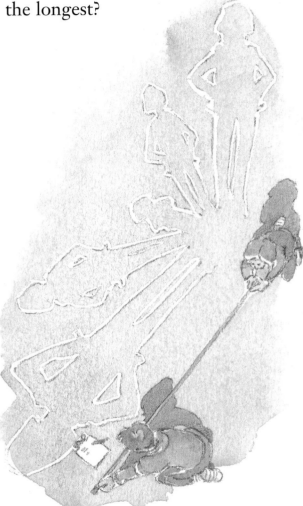

You should observe that your friend's shadow is shortest in the middle of the day and longest near sunrise and sunset.

Try this project again in a different season. You'll find that the shadow is shortest in summer because the Sun is highest in the sky.

What is a sundial?

A sundial is a clock that uses the Sun to tell time. The pointer on the sundial casts a shadow onto a disk that has lines marked on it. These markings each have a time of day written beside them. As the Earth turns, throughout the day, the pointer's shadow moves across the disk. If the shadow falls on the line marked 11, then it is 11:00 in the morning.

The early Egyptians were the first people to discover how to use the Sun to tell time. Their sundials, or shadow clocks, were made of just a stick stuck in the ground, with lines scratched in the earth around it.

The stick is called a gnomon (say it NO-MUN) from the Greek word meaning "one who knows."